Why Do We Have Trials?

BY HAL LINDSEY

ORACLE HOUSE PUBLISHING, INC.
Murrieta, California 92564

WHY DO WE HAVE TRIALS?

Copyright © 2001 by Hal Lindsey
Published by Oracle House Publishing, Inc.
P.O. Box 1131, Murrieta, California 92564

ISBN 1-931628-03-3

Printed in the United States of America.

I dedicate this book to my dear friends,

Scott and Tami Workman, whose help

has been vital to my ministry.

I also would like to commend the faith

and vision of Larry and Dianna

Crabtree that made this book possible.

CONTENTS

We live in a world of growing uncertainty and increasing instability. The average person is faced with ten times more pressure than one who lived a hundred years ago.

The emotional impact of exponential changes in almost every area of life has been enormous. The average person is experiencing trials in his life for which he is poorly equipped to cope. Christians are certainly not exempt from these trials in life. I find a lot of confusion among Christians over the following questions: "Why do Christians who are trusting and walking with God have trials?" "Is it always because of some moral failure or lack of faith?" "Shouldn't God deliver all those who are having trials if he is expressing a positive faith?" "Why doesn't God heal every ill Christian who trusts Him?" "Is it ever God's will for a Christian to be sick?" "Is it God's will for every Christian who tithes to be wealthy?" "If I am poor, does it mean that there is something wrong with my faith?"

I have searched the Bible for answers to these and related questions for many years. This book sets forth what God showed me in His Word while in the midst of my own trials. I pray it will be a blessing to you. It may not answer every question, but hopefully, it will help you on the road to inner peace and faith in God's perfect will for your life.

Most Christians Are In "Denial"

> **Consider it pure joy, my brothers, whenever you face trials of many kinds, because you know that the testing of your faith develops perseverance.** —James 1:2-3

This Scripture sounds too "other-wordly" for a great many Christians today. It is very easy for Christians to slip into the prevailing attitude of our present world. The current mind-set is to avoid pain of any kind at any cost, to live life for the moment and ignore the long-term consequences. The principle of enduring hardship for the present to achieve a long-term future reward is virtually non-existent.

There are two extremes that Christians should avoid when approaching the subject of trials. The first is to think that God in His desire to see us grow will constantly bombard us with trials. The other is to think that there will be no trials in the life of someone who has real faith and walks with God.

Need We Fear Trials?

In answer to the first extreme, the LORD expressly promises that He will never puts us through any trial that is beyond our maturity level to endure. The LORD explains this in the following promise,

> *"No temptation has seized you except what is common to man. But God is faithful; he will not let you be tempted beyond what you can bear. But when you are tempted, he will also provide a way out so that you can stand up under it."*
> (1 Corinthians 10:13)

Nor does He give us more testing than is necessary to train our faith for our particular calling. The Bible clearly shows that *all those who are greatly used are greatly tested*. And in these cases the LORD gives such grace that the one who is so tested is filled with inner joy while in the midst of his trials.

The Case Of Paul And Silas

Just look at Paul and Silas' experience at Philippi (see Acts 16:11-40). They were totally committed to their mission of founding new churches. They were walking by faith and were in the city of Philippi by the direct leading of the LORD Jesus Himself. They had courageously witnessed in the face of dangerous opposition.

After much sacrificial labor, they had only two converts—a traveling saleswoman and a formerly demon-possessed fortune-telling slave girl. As a result of delivering the slave girl from her demon of fortune telling, her master had them arrested, brutally beaten with the Roman cat-o'-nine-tails and thrown into the lower dungeon of the jail. The lower dungeons were usually filthy, wet, and filled with large rats.

How would you have responded to this situation? Most of us would have sunk into a massive depression and self-pity. We would probably have said, "LORD, I don't deserve this. There I was, boldly witnessing for You. I barely had enough to eat. I was walking with all my heart in obedience to Your Word. And to top it all off, I came here because You appeared to me in a vision and told me to come. And after all this sacrifice, You let me get my back beaten to shreds and my body put into chains in this lousy dungeon so that I can't even fight off the rats. I thought you loved me. This isn't fair?"

Supernatural From An Unnatural Response

But what did Paul and Silas do? With their backs raw and bleeding, their muscles aching from being chained in an uncomfortable position in a damp dungeon, *they sang praises to the LORD at the top of their voices!* And the LORD answered this incredible display of combat faith with an earthquake that shook the whole region, shattered their chains, and flung open the prison doors. Praise Jesus, one way or another He will always respond to His children who praise Him in the midst of unexplainable trials.

As a result, the head jailer, all his family, and most of the prisoners came to know the LORD Jesus as their Savior. All of these became the charter members of the Philippian Church, which became characterized by rejoicing in the midst of trials. It was all made possible because Paul and Salas walked by faith and not by sight. They believed the promise, *"We know that God causes all things to work together for good to those who love God, to those who are called according to His purpose."* (Romans 8:28) All things are not good, but when we believe

God, He makes even the bad things work together for good.

This incident illustrates how those who are tested for the ministry's sake are given special grace, if they trust the LORD. Those who are so tested are not miserable and frightened, but excited and filled with inner joy, sensing the LORD's personal presence, knowing that their life is counting for eternity.

Do Committed Christians Have Trials?

This is a hard question to answer because of the teaching of some popular contemporary ministers. Most Christians of this generation are in "an attitude of denial" about the subject of trials. This is the second extreme that must be avoided. No one wants to have trials, and certainly no one should seek them. But the Bible is filled with accounts about its greatest people of faith suffering trials, not the least of whom is Jesus Himself. The Bible clearly shows that it's greatest heroes of faith suffered trials. God's Hall of Fame, Hebrews Chapter 11, is a prime example of this.

Some ministers with great followings teach that if you are truly living with a "positive confession of faith", you will not experience trials, especially a trial that involves physical illness. This teaching attributes virtually all trials, suffering, sickness, and poverty to a lack of faith or some un-confessed sin. While it is true that these conditions do bring about trials, they are certainly not the cause of all trials. This teaching ignores a large part of the Scripture in order to establish a doctrine of "easy going discipleship". No one is going to be used of God without a BD degree—a "Backside of the Desert" degree. Just ask Moses at "moses@exodus.com."

It is difficult to combat these teachers because they mix a lot of truth with a touch of error. *It is true that God wants us to have a positive confession of faith. But it must be expressed with the right personal motives in accordance with God's revealed will.* If you persist in a positive confession of faith over something that is not God's will, then God help you if He gives it to you. I have seen some believers beg God to take back "answers to their positive confession" that turned out to be not His will. If we persist in begging God for things with fleshly motives, He sometimes gives them to us in order to teach us a lesson.

Why Do We Have Trials?

We must always filter a teaching through the grid of *all* the Bible has to say on the subject. The purpose of this booklet is to present all that the Bible has to say on the subject of trials, not just selected-proof texts to fit a popular presupposition that fits the mood of this present era. I am afraid that Christians of past eras would be ashamed of us in this Laodicean era.

Focusing On God's Love

We must always remember that overriding every circumstance that touches our lives is God's deep love and compassion for each one of us. Remember how much grace and love the LORD demonstrated toward the Israelites of the Exodus even though they continued to disbelieve His promises. In reality, they always believed the worst about God's character. In spite of this, God kept delivering them and providing for their every need.

Listen to how the Psalmist perceived the enormity of God's love for the Exodus generation—even in the midst of their rebellion,

> *For they did not believe in God*
> *Or trust in His deliverance.*

Yet He gave a command to the skies above
*   And opened the doors of the heavens;*
He rained down manna for the people to eat,
*   He gave them the grain of heaven...*
In spite of all this, they kept on sinning;
In spite of His wonders,
*   They did not believe.*
Yet He was merciful;
He atoned for their iniquities
*   And did not destroy them.*
Time after time He restrained His anger
*   And did not stir up his full wrath.*
He remembered that they were but flesh...
    —Psalms 78:22-24, 32, 38-39

The Eternal Perspective

The Father always views our lives from the perspective of eternity. Our natural perspective of life, unless God changes it, is dominated by the needs and concerns of this world. One of the major characteristics of spiritual maturity is to see your life from the divine viewpoint instead of the human viewpoint. And an integral part of the divine viewpoint is to see your life through the perspective of eternity.

Christianity has been heavily criticized in our era for promising "pie in the sky by and by." Karl Marx emphasized this kind of reasoning when he called religion "the opiate of the people." He looked on Christians with contempt because he felt they passively endured sufferings and didn't fight for a better material world. He felt that the Christian faith contributed to their passive acceptance of oppression by "the rich capitalists." The record of history, however, shows that men committed to Christian ethics and morality brought about the greatest reforms and improvements for the poor of the industrial age. Christians are taught to change what they can and to accept by faith what they can't. Communism just exchanged one form of dictatorship for another. Communism's doctrine of the "end justifies the means" justified the murder of tens of millions of innocent people in order to set up their "worker's paradise." No other doctrine has ever brought about the murder of so many people. Hitler's Third Reich was moderate compared to the hell instituted by the likes of Lenin, Stalin and Mao Tze-dung.

Still Christianity does, without apology, primarily base its hope on eternity and not on this life. God said through the Apostle Paul, *"If only for this life we have hope in Christ, we are to be pitied more than all men."* (1 Corinthians 15:19) Frankly, without the perspective of eternity, I would have to conclude that much of the suffering I have witnessed *is* unfair.

Two Perspectives Of Life

We must learn to live in the reality of the fact that we are already citizens of eternity bound for a heavenly reward that is wonderful beyond human comprehension. According to God's promise, the best this life has to offer cannot even be compared to the believer's life in eternity. *"But as it is written: 'Eye has not seen, nor ear heard, nor have entered in the heart of man the things which God has prepared for those who love Him.' "* (1 Corinthians 2:9 NKJV)

The LORD contrasts these two perspectives of life, one that is focused on time and the other that is focused on eternity, and gives their respective ends:

For, as I have often told you before and now say again even with tears, many live as enemies of the cross of Christ. Their destiny is destruction, their god is their stomach, and their glory is in their shame. Their mind is on EARTHLY THINGS. But our citizenship is in heaven. And we eagerly await a Savior from there, the Lord Jesus Christ, Who, by the power that enables Him to bring everything under His control, will transform our lowly bodies so that they will be like His glorious body. (Philippians 3:18-21)

This issue is so serious that if we don't learn to look at life through the perspective of eternity, we will not be able to cope with life in time.

Coping With, "What Is Fair?"

Many situations wouldn't make sense or seem fair if this life were all we had to look forward to. I will never forget experiencing just such a situation while speaking on the Rapture (a time coming when the LORD Jesus will suddenly snatch us up to meet Him in the clouds and instantaneously transform our temporal bodies into bodies exactly like His). While giving the message, I noticed a portable hospital bed rolled into the back of the Church with a nurse standing by.

After the message, I was determined to get to the back and speak with the patient in the bed. I found a young Vietnam veteran with no arms and no legs lying there. The young nurse explained that he had trusted in Christ while she read to him a copy of ***The Late Great Planet Earth¹***. I was struck by his radiant smile. He asked me, "Hal, when Jesus transforms my body, will the new one have arms and legs?" I could hardly choke back the tears as I assured him that his new body would have perfect arms and legs. His eyes filled with hope as he smiled and said, "Oh, praise the LORD. Now it isn't so bad."

One of the most inspiring and saintly persons I've ever met is Joni Eareckson Tada. She's been paralyzed from the neck down since she was a young teenager, yet her books have given hope and faith to so many people. Her condition would make no sense at all to me if it were divorced from the certainty of the rewards she will enjoy in eternity for her courageous and contagious faith.

Remember, ***"Faith is being sure of what we hope for and certain of what we do not see."*** When we

---

1 Chapter Sixteen, Hal Lindsey, *The Late Great Plant Earth* (New York: Bantam Books, 1973).

have the certainty that every trail, every moment of suffering and sorrow, every deprivation in this life, which we endure by faith through the power of the Holy Spirit, will be rewarded a thousandfold in eternity, then we can bear them with an inner joy, peace and serenity that will sustain us through anything.

Each one of us will be touched by trials at one time or another. We may then ask, "Why did God allow this to happen to me?" Trying to understand the *"why"* of a trial is often as painful as the trial itself. This is what motivated me to search the Scriptures for an answer. I spent many years seeking to discover what God says about trials. This booklet is a summary of the reasons I found in the Bible for Christian trials. I pray that it will be a blessing to many.

Cracking the Faith Barrier

Before we seek to understand reasons why we have trials, there is one foundational principle that is imperative for all of us to learn. We have no chance of living the kind of life God desires us to live without mastering this principle. I call it "cracking the faith barrier." The teacher who first introduced me to this principle literally saved my life. His name is Pastor Robert B. Thieme, Jr. of Houston, Texas. I am sure that none of the things God has accomplished in and through my life could have been possible without the lessons I learned from him. Here is the analogy that made me understand it.

When man first attempted to exceed the speed of sound, he ran into a mysterious barrier that challenged all previous knowledge and experience. As each experimental aircraft got to the edge of the speed of sound, it would begin to be buffeted by enormous forces. Control surfaces would act abnormally; sometimes even reverse their normal operation. Instruments would be shaken to pieces. The wind noise level would be thunderous, like a screaming living thing defying the pilot to crack through the "sound barrier." Pilots often referred to it as the demons that live at entrance to the speed of the sound.

Finally, a courageous and skilled pilot named Chuck Yeager; climbed aboard an experimental Bell X-1 rocket plane he dubbed "Glamorous Glynness" after his wife. He had broken several ribs the night before, but was able to hide the injury. He so wanted his chance to crack the sound barrier that no risk seemed to great for him. He had to close the cockpit cover using his good side with the help of a sawed off broom handle.

Yeager was dropped from a B29 bomber high in the stratosphere. He was thrown back against his seat as he ignited the powerful rocket engines. The little plane accelerated quickly to the edge of Mach One, the speed of sound. At Mach 0.8, the demon that lurked at the edge of the speed of sound began to buffet his plane. The buffeting was almost tearing the plane to pieces as he reported he was at Mach 0.9. Moments later, those observing from the ground heard a terrible explosion. It looked as though another brave pilot had succumbed to the sound barrier. There was some nerve wracking moments before the calm voice of Yeager reported over the radio, "Unless this Mach meter is wrong, I am doing Mach 1.2."

The experience was a shock. Immediately after the aircraft passed through the speed of sound, the buffeting stopped. There was an eerie quiet— everything was surreal and smooth in the cockpit. The wind turbulence that built up in front of every leading edge on the aircraft shifted behind it. Yeager found that it was very peaceful on the other side of the sound barrier. Future aircraft were re-designed so that the turbulence did not build up in front of the aircraft as it had before.

The Faith Barrier

Just as there is great turbulence before an aircraft cracks through the sound barrier, so there are many stresses before we learned to crack the "faith barrier." There are very definite "barriers" that blocks us from cracking through to that rarified air of living by faith in the promises of God. The barrier of trying to cope with life's trials with human strength and wisdom; the barrier of going by our emotions and feelings; the barrier of doubt; the barrier of not knowing why we are in a trial—all of these factors resist a simple trust in God.

Joy On The Other Side Of The Faith Barrier

We have to learn how to believe God's promises in spite of what our emotions and human experience tell us. There is no joy like the first time you believe a promise of God in the midst of a great trial in life and suddenly experience the "peace of God that passes all understanding" as you crack through the barrier of your emotions and doubts. The turbulence is still there, but it is shifted behind you so that God can handle it. You find an unexplainable peace on the inside that comes from really knowing that "God works all things together for good" for those who love and trust Him.

God doesn't promise us a life free of trials, but He does promise us peace on the inside in the midst of trials. That is why He has left us more than 7000 promises that cover every need we have. They are there to give us victory in whatever circumstance we find ourselves. Faith in God's promises is the most important lesson we can ever learn. I am convinced that many trials are allowed by God to help us "crack the faith barrier."

The DVP Versus The HVP

Once you have cracked the faith barrier, it is not so difficult to do it the next time. God restructures your thinking so that you can see His promises as more real than your doubts and fears. We learn to look at life from the divine viewpoint (DVP), which means to look at a trial from the perspective of God's power to deal with it through us. We learn to no longer look at life from the human viewpoint (HVP), which is to look at a trial from the perspective of our human ability to cope with it. The former gives victory, peace and joy. The latter gives defeat, misery and depression.

Discipline For Sin

One of the reasons there are trials and suffering in the Christian's life is as a discipline for personal sin. The Bible says concerning the Christian's sin, *"Anyone, then, who knows the good he ought to do and doesn't do it, sins."* And also, *"...everything that does not come from faith is sin."* (James 4:17 and Romans 14:23)

These two verses show that sin in the Christian's life is related to his present level of knowledge and faith. When we sin as a believer in one of these two ways, we break fellowship with the LORD. Sin does not sever our relationship, which is secured forever by the finished work of Christ on the cross. But sin does break our fellowship.

We remain out of fellowship until we confess our *known* sin to the LORD and trust Him again to give us victory over temptation. God promises this,

"If we (Christians) say we have no sin, we are deceiving ourselves, and the truth is not in us. If we confess our sins, He is faithful and just to forgive us our sins and to cleanse us from all unrighteousness. If we say that we have not sinned, we make Him a liar, and His word is not in us." (1 John 1:8-10)

The original verb *"to confess"* (homolegeo) means to say the same thing about sin that God does. We cannot agree with God about sin in our life that we don't understand. As the promise requires, we can only be specific and agree with God about sin we know. So God promises that if we confess what we know, *He cleanses us from all unrighteousness* of which we are unaware. In this way, God deals with us concerning our fellowship according to our level of spiritual maturity. Simply put, if we confess what we know, He forgives us what we don't know.

If we continue not to change our minds about a sin and don't confess it, then the LORD will discipline us in order to train us to walk in fellowship with Him.

The Dynamics Of The Divine "Woodshed"

This is what the Scriptures says about discipline:

And you have forgotten that word of encouragement that addresses you as sons: "My son, do not make light of the LORD's discipline, and do not lose heart when He rebukes you because the LORD disciplines those He loves, and He [corrects by scourging] everyone He accepts as a son."

Moreover, we have all had human fathers who discipline us and we respected them for it. How much more should we submit to the Father of our spirits and live! Our fathers disciplined us for a little while as they thought best; but God disciplines us for our good, [for the purpose] that we may share in His holiness. No discipline seems pleasant at the time, but painful. Later on, however it produces a harvest of righteousness and peace for those who have been trained by it. (Hebrews 12:5-11)

I want to emphasize that this is only *one* of the reasons for trials in the Christian's life. Many Christians have been taught that this is the only reason for trials. This comes out of the great error of believing that all trials and suffering are direct retribution for some act of personal sin and unbelief. This has been a part of man's thinking from earliest records. Job's "three friends" reflected this as they debated about what kind of great secret sin has brought such calamity upon him. But Job was not being disciplined because of some personal sin.

I heard one popular TV preacher say that Job suffered because of a "negative confession" of faith. This statement missed the whole point of the book of Job. The LORD Himself testified this about Job when he warned Israel of coming judgment,

> *"Or if I send a plague into that land and pour out my wrath upon it through bloodshed, killing its men and their animals, as surely as I live, declares the Sovereign LORD, even if Noah, Daniel and Job were in it, they could save neither son nor daughter. They would save only themselves by their righteousness."*
> (Ezekiel 14:19-20)

Here the LORD holds Job up along with Noah and Daniel as supreme examples of a life of faith. It is erroneous popular teaching like this that makes it so hard for believers today to understand what the Bible says about trials.

Discipline Under Grace

It is whom the LORD *loves* that He disciplines. God loves us too much to let us waste our lives out of fellowship with Him, pursuing activities that will not only make us miserable in this life, but empty-handed in eternity. From the moment we trust in Christ, we are saved forever. The Father could take us home right then. But He leaves us on this planet to share in His work of saving the lost, to train us for our eternal role as kings and priests with Christ, and to bring Him glory on earth. He gives us the precious opportunity to earn rewards that will be enjoyed for all eternity. What we do in time, echoes in eternity, as Maximus said.

For this same reason, God sometimes withholds things from us that we want and feel we should have. As a teenager, I was not able to understand why my parents were so cruel and lacking in understanding as not to let me have a motorcycle.

They were looking from a perspective that I was incapable of comprehending from my limited experience. A couple of years later, I did understand better, as I attended the funeral of a friend killed on a motorcycle. In a much greater way, The Heavenly Father looks at our lives from the vantage point of infinite wisdom and foreknowledge, guided by the desire to give us only the best.

Discipline by Grace
Versus Punishment Under Law

The LORD disciplines every child He receives because He loves him. But He doesn't punish a Christian in a harsh, punitive sense. All punishment of this sort due our sins was born once and for all by the LORD Jesus on the cross.

Discipline, on the other hand, is always forward looking and is designed to bring us back and keep us in fellowship with Christ. Punishment looks backward and repays an offender in direct proportion for his offense.

If God ever paid us back for our sins, there would be nothing left of us. On this point, the Scripture says,

He does not treat us as our sins deserve or repay us according to our iniquities. For as high as the heavens are above the earth, so great is His love for those who fear [reverently trust] Him; as far as the east is from the west, so far has He removed our transgressions from us. (Psalm 103:10-12)

Does God "Get Even" With Us?

Those who teach that God gets even with us for our sins love to use the following text to prove their point: *"Do not be deceived, God is not mocked; for whatever a man sows, this he will also reap."* (Galatians 6:7 NASB) This verse has been consistently misinterpreted by ministers to apply to the principle of Divine discipline. If this were the correct interpretation, it would contradict everything the Bible teaches on the subject. It would mean that God punishes us for sin on the basis of the principle, *"an eye for an eye and a tooth for a tooth."* (Exodus 21:24— This principle was given to judges of Israel administering the Law of Moses in a civil court. It meant that they should make the civil punishment fit the crime.)

But when we put Galatians 6:7 into its context, it clearly speaks of the principle of supporting financially those who teach us God's word. The analogy of sowing and reaping is consistently used in connection with giving money to the LORD's work (compare 1 Corinthians 9:3-18 and 2 Corinthians 9:6-15 with Galatians 6:6-10). When these Scriptures are compared and kept in context, the meaning becomes obvious.

The consistent misinterpretation of Galatians 6:6-10 shows how prone Christians are to thinking of God as vengeful rather than loving and gracious. How it must grieve the heart of our loving Father, who did not spare His own son in order to set Himself free to be gracious and merciful to us. We must beware of reading into the Bible a congenital human bias that sees the LORD as anxiously awaiting the opportunity to get even with us for our sin.

God's Four Principles For Discipline

There are four main principles to remember about Divine discipline that will help us benefit from its training more quickly.

FIRST: THE PURPOSE FOR DISCIPLINE

"God disciplines us for our good, that we may share in His holiness." (Hebrews 12:10)

Discipline is always for our benefit. The Father wants us to be truly happy and productive for eternity. His discipline is designed to teach us to live a holy life through the power of the Holy Spirit.

SECOND: DISCIPLINE IS TURNED TO BLESSING

As soon as we confess our sin and begin to believe God's promises again, He turns our discipline into blessing. The LORD's presence and comfort are immediately experienced when we believe the promises that God does not hold our sins against us. (Psalm 130:3-5)

David writes of this aspect of discipline right after confessing his awful sins of murder, adultery, and deception. Note the progression of Psalm 32, which he wrote after he was back in fellowship with the LORD.

David's renewed appreciation of eternal security:
Blessed is he whose transgressions are forgiven, whose sins are covered. Blessed is the man

**whose sin the LORD does not count against him
and in whose spirit is no deceit.**

David's remembrance of misery while out of fellowship:
When I kept silent (refusing to confess his sin)**,
my bones wasted away through my groaning all
daylong. For day and night your hand was
heavy upon me** (in Divine discipline)**; my
strength was sapped as in the heat of summer.**

David's confession and immediate forgiveness:
**Then I acknowledge my sin to You and did not
cover up my iniquity. I said, " I will confess my
transgressions to the LORD"—and You forgave
the guilt of my sin.**

David's advice to those out of fellowship:
**Therefore let everyone who is godly pray to You
while You may be found** (don't put off
confession of sin)**; surely when the mighty
waters rise** (refers to severe discipline)**, they will
not reach him.**

David's faith in God's promises:
**You are my hiding place; You will protect me
from trouble and surround me with songs of
deliverance [and praise].**

God's personal promise in response to David's faith:
I WILL instruct you and teach you in the way you should go; I WILL counsel you with My eye upon you.

David counsels us from his experience:
Do not be like the horse or the mule, which have no understanding but must be controlled...or they will not come near you.

David's testimony of God's grace to those who believe:
Many are the woes of the wicked, but the LORD's unfailing love surrounds the man who trusts in Him.

God always responds to the faith of an out of fellowship believer. It is not primarily our sin that keeps us from being used by God, but our lack of faith. When we trust the LORD, He will keep us from sin through the power of the indwelling Holy Spirit. If the average Christian were to commit the sins that David did, it is doubtful he would have the faith to believe that God could use him again. The secret of David's continued usefulness to God after this terrible period of sin is his faith as expressed in the first two verses above. He believed that God was not holding his past sins against him—and God did not.

Paul clearly speaks to the point,

> **"In a large house there are articles not only of gold and silver, but also of wood and clay; some are for noble purposes and some for ignoble. If a man cleanses himself from the latter, he will be an instrument for noble purposes, made holy, useful to the Master and prepared to do any good work."** (2 Timothy 2:20-21)

The large house is God's family. The articles of furniture illustrate believers in the family. Those who cleanse themselves by confessing their sin will be used for noble purposes and receive rewards. Those who don't will still be in the family, but without rewards.

Isn't our Father wonderful? He is the God of another chance—not just a second chance, but also another and another and another! How do we cleanse ourselves from sin? By claiming and believing the promise of 1 John 1:9.

The Imperative Of Believing Your Forgiven

David brings out an imperative truth. Once we turn to God and confess our sin, Satan goes all out to get the believer to doubt he is really forgiven. Some people even think that a guilt complex somehow helps atone for their sin. If you still feel guilty after you have confessed your sin to God, guess where that feeling is coming from. It is certainly not from God—He always keeps his Word. Satan knows that if he can get you to think that God is making a list of your sins and holding them against you, you will not be able to believe him for victory in the present.

Listen to the great lesson David, inspired by God's Spirit, teaches us,

> *If You, Lord, should mark* (keep a record of) *iniquities, O Lord, who could stand? But there is forgiveness with You, so that You may be feared* (reverently trusted). *I wait for the Lord, my soul waits, and in His word I do hope.* (Psalm 130:4-5 NKJV)

If God kept a record of our sins and held them against us, we could never have the bold faith needed to have daily victory over sin. We certainly wouldn't be able to serve Him in a vital way—because every man alive fails God badly at one time or another. Then if you don't believe God, you put yourself on the shelf through unbelief.

Post Confession Guilt Kills

I wrote about this in my booklet, *The Guilt Trip*. A prominent woman wrote me about her experiences related to this book. She shared how she had slipped into a sexual encounter with her husband's friend. She was a Church-going-Christian and had never done anything like this. She felt horrible and kept asking God to forgive her. But the guilt just kept getting worse—she was tormented day and night with it. Finally she could stand it no more. She planned her suicide so that it would appear to be an accident and not embarrass her husband and children. The day before she planned to execute her plan, she ran across a copy of *The Guilt Trip*. She read it, and thought to herself, "Can this be really true?" She then prayed and agreed with God that what she had done was sin—she also agreed with God about another thing He said— "It is forgiven." The moment she believed God's Word, the horrible burden was lifted from her. She felt like she was walking on air. Years later, that lady is still serving the Lord in a wonderful way.

Why Do We Have Trials?

THIRD: DISCIPLINE IS TEMPORARY

Once the LORD's discipline has taught us its intended lesson, it is either removed or turned into a blessing. One this point the Bible teaches: *"For His anger lasts only a moment, but His favor lasts a lifetime; weeping may remain for a night, but rejoicing comes in the morning."* (Psalm 30:5)

And again, as Jeremiah wept over the discipline of Israel,

> *"Yet this I call to mind and therefore I have hope: [It is] because of the LORD's great love we are not consumed, for His compassions never fail. They are new every morning; great is Your faithfulness...*
>
> *"Though He bring grief, He will show compassion, so great is His unfailing love. For He does not willingly bring affliction or grief to the children of men."* (Lamentations 3:21-23, 32-33)

FOURTH: TWO RESULTS OF DISCIPLINE

The result for the one who confesses his sin and trusts the LORD will be this: *"No discipline seems pleasant at the time, but painful. Later on, however, it produces a harvest of righteousness and peace for those who have been trained by it."* (Hebrews 12:11) So for this one, it produces a righteous behavior and an experience of God's peace.

The result for the one who does not trust the LORD's promises is expressed in this verse: *"See to it that no one misses that grace of God and that no root of bitterness grows upon to cause trouble and defile many."* (Hebrews 12:15) If we fail to believe God's promises, discipline will surely produce a root of bitterness that opens the door for Satan to enter our life. Then we will not only fall into greater sin, but cause many others to stumble as well.

Trials To Keep Us From Pride

The Scripture says that some trials are allowed into our lives to keep us from falling into pride. Pride was the original sin that caused Lucifer to fall and become Satan. God put pride at the top of the list of sins He hates,

> *"These six things the Lord hates, Yes, seven are an abomination to Him: A PROUD LOOK, a lying tongue, hands that shed innocent blood, a heart that devises wicked plans, feet that are swift in running to evil, a false witness who speaks lies, and one who sows discord among brethren."* (Proverbs 6:13-16)

Because of this, the LORD takes special precautions to keep His servants from falling into this "snare of the Devil."

The sin of pride is a particular temptation for the servant of Christ who is given great spiritual gifts and understanding of God's Word. Listen to what the Apostle Paul shared concerning this:

> *To keep me from becoming conceited because of these surpassingly great revelations, there was given me a thorn in my flesh, a messenger of Satan, to torment me. Three times I pleaded with the LORD to take it away from me. But He said to me, "My grace is sufficient for you, for My power is made perfect in weakness." Therefore I will boast all the more gladly about my weakness, so that Christ's power may rest on me. That is why, for Chris's sake, I delight in weakness, in insults, in hardships, in persecutions, in difficulties. For when I realize I am weak, then I am truly strong.*
> (2 Corinthians 12:7-10)

There is some debate over what exactly Paul meant by the *"thorn in his flesh"* and *"weakness."* Whatever it was, it caused torment to Paul's body. Most careful Bible expositors believe that this was a very painful and troublesome eye disease, resulting from Paul's blinding vision of

Why Do We Have Trials?

the LORD Jesus on the road to Damascus. Perhaps the chronic eye problem served as a constant reminder to Paul of how he was made blind so that he could see the truth.

The word translated weakness is from the Greek verb ασθενεω. Its primary meaning is "to be ill or physically sick". Its secondary meaning is "weakness." The Greeks believed that all sickness stemmed from a weakness in the body. Today we find that's pretty accurate. Most sickness does stem from a weakness in the immune system.

Timothy's Frequent Illnesses

This same word is used to describe Timothy's condition, ***"Stop drinking only water, and use a little WINE because of your stomach and your FREQUENT ILLNESSES."*** (1 Timothy 5:23 NIV) Paul praised Timothy for his faithfulness, dependability and Spirit-led service. These frequent illnesses were not for discipline or lack of faith. If it were God's will to heal him, why didn't Paul send a blessed handkerchief to heal him, as he did on an occasion in the book of Acts? But instead he told him to drink some fermented wine, which was free from harmful bacteria (Sorry Baptists). It is obvious to the unprejudiced reader that God had some greater purpose in Timothy's frequent illnesses related to his stomach. There is no rebuke for any failure on Timothy's part.

Paul's Illness Spread Gospel To Galatia

The following passage indicated Paul's problem,

> *"As you know it was because of an illness that I first preached the gospel to you. Even though my illness was a trial to you, you did not treat me with contempt or scorn... I can testify that, if you could have done so, you would have torn out your eyes and given them to me."* (Galatians 3:13-15)

We can draw the following conclusions from this passage:

First, the illness must have involved Paul's eyes or else the statement that the Galatians would have been willing, if possible, to give Paul their eyes would not make sense.

Why Do We Have Trials?

Second, the condition must have made Paul look so repulsive that it was a trial for them at first to receive him.

Third, God used the flare-up of Paul's eye disease to force him to stay long enough in the Province of Galatia to preach the gospel to them.

Fourth, this should answer the inaccurate contention on the part of some that say God never allows sickness into the life of a Christian who believes Him and walks with Him. God uses Paul's illness to guide him into evangelizing the vast region of Galatia, which he apparently would otherwise have bypassed. So this illness was clearly in the will of God for Paul.

The Importance Of Knowing You Are Weak

I believe that God desires to and does heal us, but there are cases, as illustrated here, where He has a greater purpose to accomplish. Once again, we must remember God looks at each situation from the standpoint of eternity. There are some cases where you can pray until you're blue in the face and there will be no healing. We must seek the LORD's will in all our prayers, not merely our own world-influenced will. But of this we can be certain: If a person who is ill has confessed every known sin in his life, and if the LORD does not immediately heal him, then the LORD in His love and wisdom has a greater purpose that perhaps we may not understand in this life, but that will certainly count for all eternity.

God used Paul's eye illness (and possibly other physical afflictions) not only to keep Paul from pride, but also to keep him aware of the weakness and inadequacy of human ability to accomplish His work. This caused Paul to depend constantly on the Holy Spirit to fill and empower his life. This is why he said, ***"When I realize I am weak, then I am strong."*** When we realize that in our human ability we are weak, and then depend completely upon the Holy Spirit, His power accomplishes the impossible.

Paul pleaded with the LORD in three specific prayer sessions to take his physical illness away, but the LORD clearly showed him the greater purpose in it—to keep him from being ensnared by pride. After that, Paul not only accepted the bodily affliction, but also embraced it as God's will.

We may be missing a greater blessing in an affliction simply because we refuse to accept God's purpose in it. Rather than learning how to be strong through realizing our weakness as Paul did, we often, like spoiled children, demand an instant removal of all afflictions.

Trials To Build Faith

The experiences of the Exodus generation are among God's greatest historical lessons for teaching us how He uses trials to make us crack the faith barrier.

Peter spoke of this purpose for trials when he said,

> ***In this*** (salvation) ***you greatly rejoice; even though now for a little while, if necessary, you have been distressed by various trials, [for the purpose] that the proof of your FAITH, being more precious than gold which is perishable, even though tested by fire, may be found to result in praise and glory and honor at the revelation of Jesus Christ.*** (1 Peter 1:6-7 NASB)

Faith Proven By Fire

The Greek term, δοκιμιον from δοκιμη, which is translated proof, means, "to put something to the test for the purpose of proving its genuineness." The comparison of the proving of faith to the method of purifying gold gives a graphic illustration. Gold is purified by heating it to a molten state over fire. This causes all the impurities to rise to the top. Then the impurities can easily be raked off. The fire of trials causes the impurities of a believer's faith to be cleansed in the same way.

Just examine the lives of all the men of the Bible who served God in a might way—Moses, David, Job, Daniel, and the Apostles, to name a few. All of those men had their faith tried and proven by fire of trials allowed into their lives.

Paul the apostle single-handedly took the Gospel of Christ to the outer limits of the Roman Empire in his lifetime. And he did this without any means of modern transportation or communication. No one has ever equaled that performance since. Just listen to the message the LORD sent to Paul when He called him;

"But the LORD told Ananias, 'Go! This man is My chosen instrument to carry My name before the Gentiles and their kings and before the people of Israel. I WILL SHOW HIM HOW MUCH HE MUST SUFFER FOR MY NAME.'" (Acts 9:15-16)

One thing for sure, this is not the way the world would enlist a CEO. And how is this statement for "a positive confession"? The LORD didn't give Paul much with which to develop a positive attitude. Some of our modern preachers would say that the LORD needed a little crash course in how to promote "positive thinking" here.

As I said before, faith is like a muscle. Just as muscle tissue gets flabby through lack of exercise, so faith gets flabby through lack of challenge. A person can develop faith through learning from the trials of the biblical heroes of faith. But combat faith is learned only by personal experience. In athletics, a muscle must be exercised to its present limit of endurance in order to grow. If you do 50 push-ups until it is easy, you will stop growing in strength unless you keep increasing the number and resistance.

Trials That Cause Growth

James, the half brother of the LORD Jesus comments on this:

> *"Consider it all joy, my brethren, when you encounter various trials, knowing that the testing of your faith produces endurance* [faith in the long run]. *And let endurance have its perfect result, that you may be MATURE and complete, lacking in nothing."* (James 1:2-4 NASB)

Here, various trials produce a special kind of faith, which brings about overall spiritual maturity. The chief characteristic of maturity is faith. This special faith is called endurance, which is a faith that persists and doesn't give up when deliverance is delayed.

Job demonstrated this kind of faith under undeserved and unexplained trial when he said,

"Though He slay me, yet will I trust in Him." (Job 13:15)

Faith And Muscle Develop Similarly

The development of faith is often compared to athletics in the Bible, and with very good reason. The Bible likens the Christian life to running a race: ***"...let us run with endurance the race that is set before us. Fixing our eyes on Jesus, the author and perfecter of [our] faith."*** (Hebrews 12:1-2) The idea is that God wants distance runners, not sprinters, in this race of living by faith. God wants "faith muscle" that can endure under extended stress. He doesn't want "faith muscle" that gives a short burst of performance but cannot endure. Some Christians are like sprinters: they believe the LORD for a short while in a showy burst of faith—and then fall apart. God wants those who keep on believing and leaning upon Him even though the trials persist. This is what God calls a truly mature faith.

Paul also commented on the trials that bring about maturity,

> ***"Not only so, but we also rejoice in our sufferings, because we know that***

suffering produces perseverance; perseverance, proven character; and proven character hope. And hope does not disappoint us, because God has poured out His love into our hearts by the Holy Spirit, whom He has given us." (Romans 5:3-5)

It isn't that God is trying to produce a bunch of spiritual masochists, but rather that for a limited time, certain trials are necessary to produce growth and proven character. But the LORD reminds us that His love is made especially manifest to us during these times through the indwelling Holy Spirit. He lavishly pours out His love within us, so that we are sustained in a special way by it.

Trials That Teach Obedience

All the biblical heroes of faith who were used significantly first went through a period of testing and training.

As we analyze some of God's greatest servants, we discover that all went through tests and trials not because of some personal sin, but because god wanted to strengthen their personal discipline so that they could withstand Satan's attacks. The more God uses us, the more of a target of Satan we become.

The greatest example is the LORD Jesus Christ Himself. The writer to the Hebrews spoke of this:

> *In the days of His life on earth, He offered up both prayers and supplications with loud crying and tears to the One able to deliver Him out of death* [i.e., He was

resurrected], *and He was heard because of His humble submission. Although He was a Son He learned obedience from the things which He suffered.* (Hebrews 5:7-8)

Jesus, the Son of God, is the most unique person in the universe. He is both absolute God and true humanity united in one person forever. It is in His true human nature that He was trained in obedience and discipline. As soon as Jesus started His public ministry, His discipline of faith and obedience to the Father were severely tested by the Devil (see Luke 4:1-8)

Paul is another example. The Lord Jesus' command to Ananias when he was sent to speak to Paul (who was then know as the dangerous Saul of Tarsus) was,

> *"Go, for he is a chosen instrument of Mine, to bear My name before the Gentiles and kings and the sons of Israel; for I will show him how much he must suffer for My name's sake."* (Acts 9:15-16 NASB)

As I said before, this is not the way the world would recruit one of its chief leaders, is it? The problem is, both Christians and those in the world fail to realize that it is possible to be content and full of joy even in the midst of trials. This is the testimony that Paul later gave:

> *But I rejoice in the LORD greatly. Not that I speak from want; for I have learned to be content in whatever circumstances I am. I know how to get along with humble means, and I also know how to live in prosperity; in any and every circumstance I have learned the secret of being filled and going hungry, both of having abundance and suffering need. I can do all things through Christ who keeps on strengthening me.* (Philippians 4:11-13 HL)

Not everyone will go through this kind of trial. Still, there is a principle involved: the Greater the mission, the greater need for training in obedience and discipline. This is why Jesus cautioned those who wanted to follow Him into a position of leadership to first count the cost. It has been the greatest thrill of my life to be used by God, but there is a cost. It is not a burden if you know the reason for the trials that come to prepare you for service.

REASON SIX
Trials That Keep Us From Sin

Our heavenly Father knows that we all have an old sin nature that has certain areas of weakness that make us vulnerable to particular temptations. So God, In His faithfulness as a loving Father, allows certain trials into our lives to prevent us from being trapped by our areas of weakness.

Peter comments on this vital truth,

> *Therefore, since Christ suffered in his body, arm yourselves also with the same attitude, because he who has suffered in his body is done with sin. As a result, he does not live the rest of his earthly life for evil human desires, but rather for the will of God. For you have spent enough time in the past doing what pagans choose to do—living in debauchery, lust, drunkenness, orgies, carousing and*

***detestable idolatry. They think it strange
that you do not plunge with them into the
same flood of dissipation, and they heap
abuse on you.*** (1 Peter 4:1-4 NIV)

Trials directed by the loving hand of God
prevent us from being susceptible to our areas
of weakness. Suffering also encourages us to
pursue God's will for our lives, because it takes
our mind off the trivial things of this life and
focuses it on the things of God.

I have discipled so many super-talented young
men who would have been drawn astray by the
things of this world if the LORD had not gotten
their attention through trials. God also broke the
hold that certain areas of the sin nature had
upon me, by putting me through trials that kept
me from falling into those areas.

Just as Paul was kept from falling into pride
through a painful affliction, so suffering keeps
us back from the areas of weakness in our old
sin nature.

Trials That Equip Us To Comfort Others

Some trials give us the ability to have maximum empathy for those who are in a similar situation we have experienced:

> *"Blessed be the God and Father of our Lord Jesus Christ, the Father of mercies and God of all comfort; Who comforts us in all our affliction SO THAT we may be able to comfort those who are in any affliction with the comfort with which we ourselves are comforted by God."*
> (2 Corinthians 1:3-4)

Let's take one example: There is no one who can comfort someone who has lost a loved one as well as a person who has been comforted by the LORD in the same experience. This person can share with such conviction and power how God comforted him in his sorrow that it will inspire faith and comfort in the grieving one.

Those who have great ministries of counseling and showing mercy usually have had a number of personal trials. This gives them an insight, understanding, and empathy that can be gained in no other way.

Trials That Prove The Reality Of Christ In Us

The supernatural life of Christ lived out through a Christian is most manifest when a believer through faith undergoes trials with a supernatural attitude of praise and joy. This is the result of the Holy Spirit producing the inner joy and characteristics of the indwelling Christ in us. This is so contrary to normal human behavior that the unbeliever is confronted with the reality of the Christ we proclaim.

A man named Stephen was of the first Christian to demonstrate the power of the Holy Spirit to produce Christ in us. After giving one of the greatest messages in the New Testament, he was taken out and stoned to death. But the one who had arrested and brought charges against him, Saul of Tarsus, never forgot what he saw in Stephen during his trial and cruel death. Stephen was so filled with the Holy Spirit that they first saw this, ***"And fixing their gaze upon him***

(Stephen), *all who were sitting in the Council* (Sanhedrin) *saw his face as the face of an angel.*" (Acts 6:15) There is only one person who could have been an eyewitness and later told Luke about it—Saul of Tarsus, who became the Apostle Paul.

It was also undoubtedly Paul who witnessed the execution of Stephen and later reported the amazing way that Stephen died,

> *"And they went on stoning Stephen as he called upon the Lord and said, 'Lord Jesus, receive my spirit!' And falling on his knees, he cried out with a loud voice, 'Lord, do not hold this sin against them!' And having said this, he fell asleep."* (Acts 7:59-60)

Stephen manifested the very character of Christ as he died. This so got to Saul of Tarsus that it started him on the road of conviction. It is fascinating that Paul's style of preaching became much the same as what he heard from Stephen.

Paul frequently taught about Christ being revealed in us, *"My children, with whom I am again in labor until Christ is formed in you ...* " (Galatians 4:19) Again, he spoke of the Holy Spirit's ministry of producing the life of Christ in us: ***"But we have this treasure in earthen vessels, that the surpassing greatness of the power may be*** (demonstrated to be) ***of God and not from ourselves."*** (2 Corinthians 4:7 NASB) Then Paul writes of how this treasure of Christ's life in him was lived out in his experiences:

> ***We are hard pressed on every side but not crushed; perplexed, but not in despair; persecuted, but not abandoned; struck down, but not destroyed. We also carry around in our body the death of Jesus, SO THAT THE LIFE OF JESUS MAY ALSO BE REVEALED IN OUR BODY. For we who are alive are always being given over to death for Jesus' sake, SO THAT HIS LIFE MAY BE REVEALED IN OUR MORTAL BODY.*** (2 Corinthians 4:8-11)

Paul's point is that Christ's life is revealed to the world through our supernatural response to our trials and tribulations. When the world sees us act totally contrary to human nature, they are attracted to find out why. Then you can lead them to faith in Christ.

REASON NINE
Trials That Glorify God

There are many examples of this kind of trial. One that inspires me most is the case of the three young Hebrew men named Shadrach, Meshach, and Abednego. In a day when most Hebrews taken as prisoners to Babylon after the destruction of Jerusalem were compromising their faith in the LORD, these three brought great glory to God by the tenacity and boldness of their faith in the face of a horrible death.

King Nebuchadnezzar built a ninety-foot-tall idol of gold and decreed that when the royal band played, all would be required to fall down and worship it. Those disobedient would be thrown into a great blazing furnace.

Some jealous court astrologers reported to the king that certain Jews he had appointed over his affairs of state refused to bow down and worship the idol. In a furious rage, Nebuchadnezzar called the three young Jews in and asked them if in fact they had refused to worship his idol.

Observe their bold faith in their reply:

> *O Nebuchadnezzar, we do not need to defend ourselves before you in this matter. If we are thrown into the blazing furnace, the God we serve is able to save us from it, and He will rescue us from your hand, O king. But even if He does not, we want you to know, O king, that we will not serve your gods or worship the image of gold you have set up.* (Daniel 3:16-18)

The king, infuriated by their answer, ordered the great blazing furnace heated seven times hotter than ever before.

So Shadrach, Meshach, and Abednego, securely bound, were thrown into the great furnace. The flames were so intense that the heat killed the men who carried out the sentence. It was at this point that the young Jews' faith brought great glory to God. The Scripture reports:

> *The King Nebuchadnezzar leaped to his feet in amazement and asked his*

advisers, "Wasn't it three men that we tied up and threw into the fire?" They replied, "Certainly, O king." He said, "Look! I see four men walking around in the fire unbound and unharmed, and the fourth looks like a son of the gods." (Daniel 3 24-25)

What a picture this paints! The only thing that we lose in our God-given trials is the thing that binds us. And the Son of God makes Himself especially near and intimate during these times.

This so impressed the king that he not only promoted these three young men of faith, but also passed a decree that no one could speak evil of their God on pain of death. Then he later came to believe in the God of Israel as his God.

Our God has not changed. The LORD will still perform mighty miracles for His glory's sake and to reveal Himself, as He sovereignly wishes.

All the martyrs of the faith, such as Stephen, brought glory to God through this kind of trial. God didn't miraculously save the martyrs as he did Shadrach, Meshach, and Abednago, but their special white robes will shine for all eternity as a brilliant testimony of their faith.

Why A Man Was Born Blind

The Lord Jesus also spoke about this kind of trial:

> *As Jesus went along, he saw a man blind from birth. His disciples asked him, "Rabbi, who sinned, this man or his parents, that he was born blind?" "Neither this man nor his parents sinned," said Jesus, "but this happened so that the work of God might be displayed in his life."* (John 9:1-3 NIV)

The disciples were following the contemporary teaching of the Religious leaders. They believed that all sickness and deformities were the result of personal sin. But Jesus shocked them by saying that it was not caused by either the blind man's or his parents' sin. Jesus taught that the man was born blind so that God's power might be displayed in him. So here is a case where God made a person physically deformed for the purpose of displaying His glory.

Was This Fair?

We might ask, "Was it fair to cause a man to suffer from birth with such a deformity?" If this life is all there is, we might say it wasn't fair. But just look at what happened. Jesus walked up to the blind man, made clay of his spittle and smeared it on his eyes, then told him to go wash his eyes in the Pool of Siloam—which means, "The Pool of the One Who Will Be Sent". All knew this was a reference to the expectation of the coming Messiah.

When the blind man did what Jesus told him to do, he miraculously received his sight on the spot. No one, particularly the religious leaders, believed this was the same blind man they had seen begging for years. It is interesting that Jesus deliberately picked the Sabbath Day to do this miracle. Jesus used this incident to expose the falseness and hypocrisy of the whole religious system. And the blind man was privileged to be a vital part of this Divine mission.

The religious leaders thoroughly interrogated the man on how he was healed and sought to intimidate him. They even called in his parents to verify that he was indeed their son that was born blind.

Then they called him in again, as if they had received new evidence against Jesus. Note the boldness and wisdom God gives his new child:

So a second time they called the man who had been blind, and said to him, "Give glory to God; we know that this man is a sinner." He therefore answered, "Whether He is a sinner, I do not know; one thing I do know, that, whereas I was blind, now I see." They said therefore to him, "What did He do to you? How did He open your eyes?" He answered them, "I told you already, and you did not listen; why do you want to hear it again? You do not want to become His disciples too, do you?" And they reviled him, and said, "You are His disciple, but we are disciples of Moses. "We know that God has spoken to Moses; but as for this man, we do not know where He is from." (John 9:24-29)

The LORD begins to use His new child to reveal the blindness of Israel's spiritual leaders. Note the amazing insight the LORD gives this new convert in his answer to the religious leaders. He answers them with a perfect logical syllogism:

> *The man answered and said to them,*
> *"Well, here is an amazing thing, that you*
> *do not know where He is from, and yet He*
> *opened my eyes.*

MAJOR PREMISE
> *"We know that God does not hear sinners;*
> *but if anyone is God-fearing, and does*
> *His will, He hears him."*

MINOR PREMISE
> *"Since the beginning of time it has never*
> *been heard that anyone opened the eyes*
> *of a person born blind."*

CONCLUSION
> *"If this man were not from God, He could*
> *do nothing." (John 9:30-33)*

This is the perfect logic of the Holy Spirit. The religious leaders had to agree with both the minor and the major premise, so he slams the irrefutable conclusion on them.

When people have no answer to a person's argument, they attack the person:

To this they replied, "You were steeped in sin at birth; how dare you lecture us!" And they threw him out. (John 9:30 NIV)

God Rewards Those Who Suffer For Him

When they cast this new believer out, Jesus went after him and gave him a reward that any believer would suffer to receive. There are very few cases in the Gospels were Jesus personally revealed to a person who He really is. This man who was born blind was given that high privilege:

> *Jesus heard that they had put him out; and finding him, He said, "Do you believe in the Son of Man?" He answered and said, "And who is He, Lord, that I may believe in Him?" Jesus said to him, "You have both seen Him, and He is the one who is talking with you." And he said, "Lord, I believe." And he worshiped Him.*
> (John :35-38)

I know that if we were to ask the man born blind if he was treated fairly, he would reply that he overwhelmingly was. He is in the eternal Word of God. He was used of God to refute the wrong teachings of some of the most brilliant men who ever lived. He has been rewarded in Heaven forever. I believe that this is why the Apostle Paul wrote:

> *Therefore we do not lose heart. Though outwardly we are wasting away, yet inwardly we are being renewed day by day. For our light and momentary troubles are achieving for us an eternal glory that far outweighs them all. So we fix our eyes not on what is seen, but on what is unseen. For what is seen is temporary, but what is unseen is eternal.* (2 Corinthians 4:16-18 NIV)

Trials That Testify To Angels

I am convinced that God chooses only very special believers for this kind of trial. There is one book in the Bible dedicated to this particular trial and it's purpose. The book of Job pulls back the veil of heaven and takes us behind the scenes to reveal an awesome conflict that exists there between God and His angels versus Satan and his fallen angels.

The Scriptures reveal:

> *"One day the angels came to present themselves before the LORD, and Satan also came with them. The LORD said to Satan, 'Where have you come from?'*
>
> *"Satan answered the LORD, 'from roaming through the earth and going back and forth in it.'"* (Job 1:6-7)

Satan's answer was deliberately insolent. He boasted to God of his ownership of the earth. Adam betrayed God when he forfeited the title deed of the earth and all it contained to Satan.

In reply, God challenged Satan, saying there was one man on earth that he didn't control. The LORD said to Satan, ***"Have you considered My servant Job? There is no one on earth like him; he is blameless and upright, a man who fears God and shuns evil."*** (Job 1:8)

Satan told the LORD that the only reason Job followed Him was because He had protected and blessed him so much. Satan challenged God: ***"Stretch out Your hand and strike everything he has, and he will surely curse You to Your face."*** (Job 1:11)

The LORD accepted the challenge and gave Satan permission to destroy everything that Job had without touching Job himself. This Satan did with a vengeance. He destroyed all of his possessions and killed all of his children. He then timed the news of all these disasters so that the reports came in one after another. This gave maximum impact to the horrible news.

Job continued to trust in the LORD even though the tests got so severe he was driven almost out of his mind. Later the LORD restored all that he had lost many-fold.

The main purpose of the book of Job is to show that God's judgment of Satan and his angels was just. Job, compared to the angels was a vastly inferior creature in intelligence and knowledge of God, yet he chose to believe in and follow the LORD despite tremendous adversity. This demonstrates that Satan, with his superior attributes and a full intimate knowledge of God, has no excuse for rebelling against Him.

God's Revelation to the Angels

Many times trials of a lesser degree are allowed into the life of a believer in order to demonstrate this same point. Angels continue to constantly observe how believers react to trials. Every aspect of god's dealing with mankind is teaching the angelic realm more about the wonder of God's infinite character.

The Apostle Paul spoke of this when he explained the purpose of his ministry and the wonder of God's grace,

Although I am less than the least of all God's people, this grace was given me: to preach to the Gentiles the unsearchable riches of Christ, and to make plain to everyone the administration of this mystery, which for ages past was kept hidden in God, who created all things. His intent was that now, through the church, the manifold wisdom of God should be made known to the rulers and authorities in the heavenly realms (high ranking officials of the angels), *according to His eternal purpose which He accomplished in Christ Jesus our Lord.* (Ephesians 3:8-11)

According to this, God is teaching the angels about His manifold wisdom, particularly through His dealings with the Church. Before "Operation Man," there was no occasion for angels to see God's attributes of love, justice, and wisdom fully demonstrated. But with the creation of man and his consequent rebellion, these attributes of God's character have been beautifully demonstrated. Above all, the infinite beauty and wonder of God's grace has been revealed to both the unfallen and fallen angels.

A Word In Job's Defense

A few ministers today teach that the reason Job suffered such trials was because of his "negative confession" when he said, ***"What I feared has come upon me; what I dreaded has happened to me."*** (Job 3:25) I believe God will make these men apologize to Job when they get to heaven. To make a statement like this is to demonstrate a complete lack of understanding of the purpose of the book of Job. It also reveals that they are ignoring what is said about Job in other parts of the Bible.

God holds up Job as one of the Bible's supreme models of persevering faith under unexplained trials in the following Scriptures:

> ***"As surely as I live declares the Sovereign LORD, even if Noah, Daniel and Job were in it*** [a country consigned to Divine judgment] ***they could save neither son nor daughter. They would save only themselves by their righteousness."*** (Ezekiel 14:20)

> ***Brothers, as an example of patience in the face of suffering, take the prophets***

who spoke in the name of the LORD. As you know, we consider blessed those who have persevered. You have heard of Job's perseverance and have seen what the LORD finally brought about. The LORD is full of compassion and mercy. (James 5:10-11)

The LORD doesn't applaud a man's faith in this way if the reason for his trials was discipline for a "negative confession." Some teachers strive so hard to make their preconceived doctrines fit the Scriptures that they twist all those verses that don't quite fit their view.

Very few, if any, will ever be called upon to suffer trials as severe as Job's, but angels learn from every situation where humans choose to believe God in the midst of trials.

Jesus' Negative Confession

Given the assumptions of the "Positive Confession" teachers, even Jesus could be accused of "negative confession." Listen to what He said:

From that time on Jesus began to explain to His disciples that He must go up to

Jerusalem and suffer many things at the hands of the elders, chief priests and teachers of the law, and that He must be killed and on the third day be raised to life. (Matthew 16:21)

Peter didn't like this at all. He was the original "positive confessor." He actually ***rebuked*** Jesus and told Him that this would never happen to Him (See Matthew 16:22). To Peter, this was a negative, defeatist confession. It didn't fit in with his ambition of being a ruler in God's kingdom, or his expectation that this would happen very soon without a lot of hardship.

Listen to what some of the "Positive Confession" teachers say, and then try to reconcile their teachings with Jesus' statement. One popular advocate of this doctrine taught, "If you confess sickness, it will develop sickness within your system. If you talk about your doubts and fears, they will become stronger. If you confess your lack of finances, it will stop the money from coming in."

Another famous advocate of "Positive Confession" wrote, "...All our words should be words of faith. We are to say only words that we want to come to pass and believe that they all will produce results. By getting into the Word of God and continually feeding on the Word so that faith controls your vocabulary, you can come to the place where all your words will come to pass." (These two statements are representative of what the "Positive Confession" movement generally believes.)

If this teaching is true, then Jesus created His own arrest, physical abuse and crucifixion by His "negative confession."

Now there is an element of truth in the 'Positive Confession' teaching. We should certainly have a positive faith. We should praise God in the midst of trials and not complain about the lack of things we don't have. *We should treat as already granted what we have believed God to do.* But before this kind of faith there should be a thorough search to find God's will in the matter.

As we examine this teaching, we should ask, who determines what is positive and/or good for our lives? Most of us would always choose a prosperous, trouble-free life that is free from any semblance of suffering and deprivation. So our "positive confessions" generally reflect that

Why Do We Have Trials?

human viewpoint. We demand that God immediately deliver us from all difficulties and suffering. We claim "our rights to wealth and prosperity." But the Bible reveals that the most important thing to consider in each one of life's circumstances is God's will. I believe in a positive confession of my faith in God's promises. But I also know that there is nothing magical about mouthing words. Nothing that pleases God will result unless I have a confidence of God's will and an understanding of why God keeps His Word. The more I know about God Himself, His faithfulness, love and power, the more I will trust in His promises.

True Faith Is Not Just 'Positive Thinking'

Peter rebuked the Lord Jesus for His "negative confession." Jesus insisted that He must go to Jerusalem to be arrested, beaten, falsely condemned and crucified. Peter in essence said, "Don't say that; I will never let this happen to you." But Jesus answered Peter in much the same way He would answer some of the "positive confessors" of today,

> *Jesus turned and said to Peter, "Out of my sight Satan! You are a stumbling block to me; you do not have in mind the things of God, but the things of men."* (Matthew 16:23)

This reflects the main flaw I have observed in the "Positive Confession" teaching. In many cases they demand the *"things of men, not the things of God."* Peter wanted a crown without a cross. Satan even tempted Jesus to take a crown without a cross. (Luke 4 1-8) This is one of his favorite tactics. The Bible presents very different expectations of life than those "Positive Confessors" generally teach. The Scriptures teach:

> *For what credit is there if, when you sin and are harshly treated, you endure it with patience? But if when you do what is right and suffer for it you patiently endure it, this finds favor with God. For you have been called for this purpose, since Christ also suffered for you, leaving you an example for you to follow in His steps...* (1 Peter 2:20-21)

The Twelfth Commandment

Let me emphasize again that God will never allow you to be tested above what you are able to stand. The LORD intends for us to enter His rest in whatever circumstance we find ourselves. As we saw through the study of God's dealing with the Exodus generation, this is possible through believing His promises.

Whether we are going through a trial, or experiencing a period of trouble-free abundance, the LORD wants us to remember His "twelfth commandment," *Thou shalt not sweat it!* (The eleventh commandment is "love others as Jesus loved you.")

Because of our hope for eternity, our sustenance and empowerment through the indwelling Holy Spirit, and the promises of God's Word for our every need, we can experience what God through James commands:

"Consider it pure joy, my brothers, whenever you face trials of many kinds, because you know that the testing of your faith develops perseverance. Perseverance must finish its work so that you may be mature and complete, not lacking anything." (James 1:2-4)

May God's miraculous work of spiritual maturity be completed in you, so that you may enjoy its rewards forever.

ABOUT THE AUTHOR

Hal Lindsey, named the best-selling author of the decade by the *New York Times*, was born in Houston, Texas. His first book, ***The Late Great Planet Earth***, published in 1970, became the best-selling nonfiction book of that decade. As of this date, he has written 20 books with a total sales of more than 35 million copies worldwide. He is one of the few authors to have three books on the *New York Times* bestseller list at the same time.

Mr. Lindsey was educated at the University of Houston. He served in the U.S. Coast Guard during the Korean War. After the service, he served as a tugboat captain on the Mississippi River. During this time Hal came to a personal faith in Christ through reading a Gideon's New Testament. Several years later, Mr. Lindsey graduated from Dallas Theological Seminary where he majored in the New Testament and early Greek literature. After completing this graduate school of theology, Mr. Lindsey served for nine years on the staff of Campus Crusade for Christ, speaking to tens of thousands of students on major university campuses throughout the United States, Canada, and Mexico.

He presently travels to speak at conferences all over the world. He continues to write books, produce videos, audio tapes and CDs.

He also anchors a weekly television news show called the *International Intelligence Briefing* on KTBN which is viewed around the world.

Want to know more?

Learn how prophecy is being fulfilled on a day to day basis? Then visit Hal Lindsey's *Oracle* online at **www.hallindsey.com**. Updated daily with the help of Jack Kinsella, *The Oracle* not only examines current world events but keeps visitors abreast with Hal Lindsey's television and radio appearances, his latest releases and provides visitors with a secure online store.

Would you like Hal Lindsey to come and give a spiritual discourse for your organization or community? ***Call* 1-800-TITUS 35** to book speaking engagements and receive more information.

Did you know that Hal Lindsey has an plethora of faith strengthening materials to help faithful Christians through these last days? ***Call* 1-800-TITUS 35 *for a free catalog*** of books, compact discs, tapes, and videos to help you maintain your spiritual armor. Or, turn the page to view a few selections from Oracle House's catalog of spiritually enriching materials available now.

WHERE IS AMERICA IN PROPHECY?

One of the most frequently asked questions by Christians today is, "Where does America fit in prophecy about the last days?" This has been a disturbing question for Hal Lindsey for more than 40 years. Here is the United States, the undisputed leader of the West since World War II, the only true Super Power in the world today, and yet it is not mentioned in the last days prophecies. But another power is clearly predicted to lead the West and then the World in the climactic events that precede the Second Coming of Jesus Christ. According to the prophets, a revived form of the old Roman people and culture, in the form of ten strong nations, will rise to take over the West. Prophets like the Apostle John and Daniel foresaw a precise scenario regarding the alignment of powers in the last days. And the U.S. is not a world leader in these predictions. The inescapable conclusion is that something catastrophic will occur specifically to America. You will not want to miss this compelling analysis of what could soon happen to the United States. ISBN 1-931628-02-5 **$21.99 plus s/h**

We are living in the last days—the evidence is all around us. *The Last Days Chronicles* is an exciting new newspaper dedicated to examining that evidence—taken directly from the daily news. Each month, you will see how what looks like chaos to the world, is proof positive that God's Plan for the human race is moving forward according to a clearly defined, pre-determined schedule.

If you would like to receive this exciting new monthly newspaper, please **call 1-800- TITUS 35**.

Suggested donation for yearly subscription $38.50.